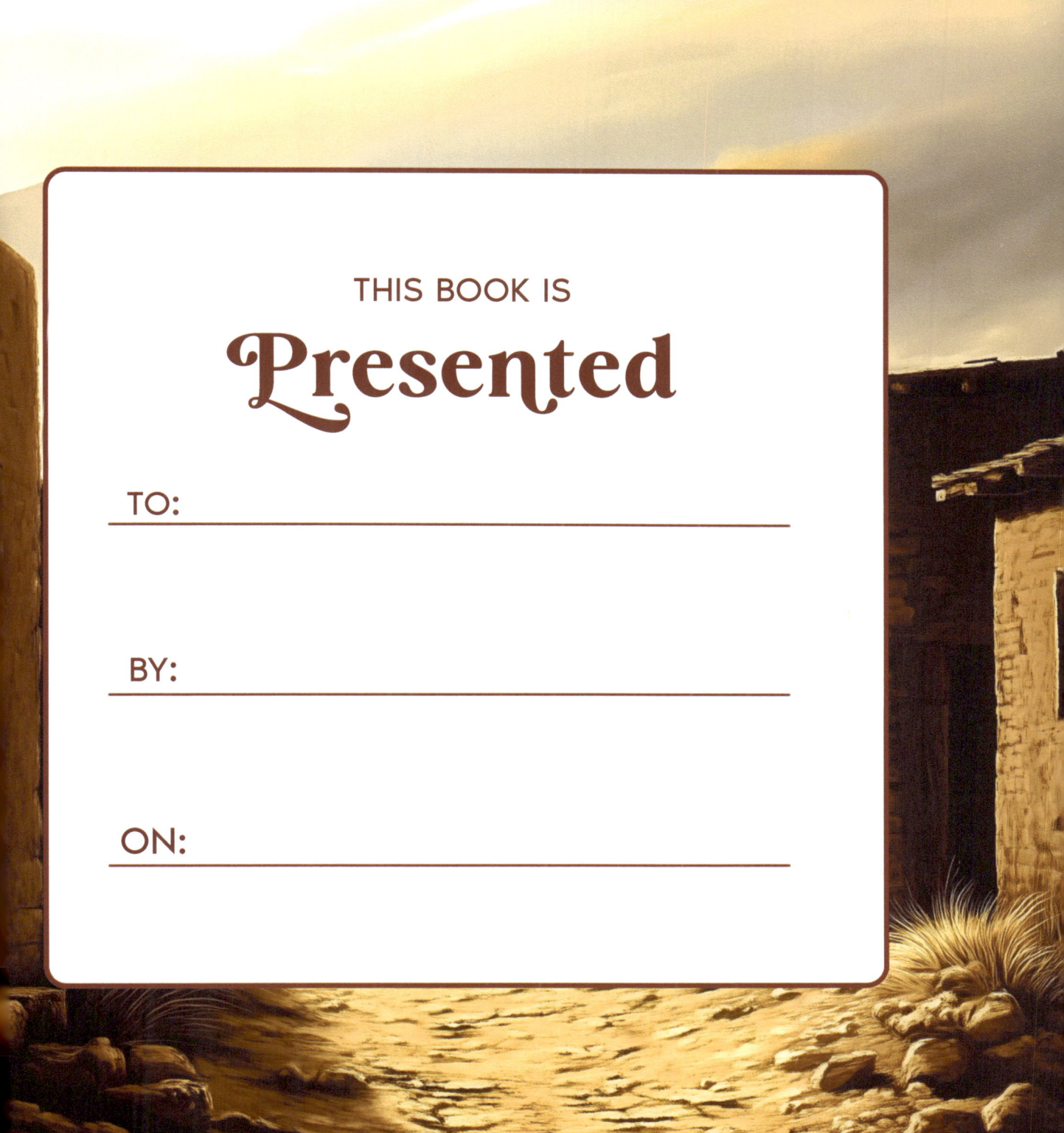

Copyright © 2025 Arabella Penrose

Arabella Penrose: Author, Art Director, Book Design
Frank S. Scavo: Poet, Story Editor, Collaborator
Tom B. Free: Artwork Editor

All rights reserved. No part of this publication may be reproduced, distributed, or transmitted in any form or by any means, or stored in any database or retrieval system, without prior written permission of the copyright holder.

All inquiries should be directed to:
www.arabellapenrose.com

ISBN-13: 978-1-962924-03-0 - Paperback
ISBN-13: 978-1-962924-10-8 - Hardcover

THE HOLY BIBLE, NEW INTERNATIONAL VERSION®, NIV® Copyright © 1973, 1978, 1984, 2011 by Biblica, Inc.® Used by permission. All rights reserved worldwide.

DEBORAH
the Prophetess

A RHYMING BIBLE STORY OF BOLD FAITH, WISE LEADERSHIP, AND TRUSTING GOD

BY ARABELLA PENROSE

"But may all who love you be like the sun when it rises in its strength."

Judges 5:31

For the young girls and boys
God is raising up as leaders in this generation.
May you be wise in your decisions,
bold for Christ, trust His victory,
and always give Him all the glory.

In Zion, long ago, there was
    a prophet in those days;
Her name was Deb'rah,
    and she led God's people in His ways.
From far and wide they came
    when justice they desired to see.
She spoke for God and judged all things
    beneath the palm, her tree.

Read: Judges 4:4-5

Read: Judges 4:1-3

But in those days, the Israelites
   did evil in God's eyes,
So, God let Canaan's ruler, Jabin,
   them to brutalize.
With his commander, Sisera,
   iron chariots they did ride.
And to the Lord for twenty years
   for help God's people cried.

Then Deb'rah rose, and to Barak
she spoke the Lord's command:
"Go! Lead ten thousand men
  to Tabor's Mount and take a stand!"
For God says, "I'll bring Sisera,
  his chariots of iron,
To Kishon River, that you may
  win victory for Zion."

Read: Judges 4:6-7

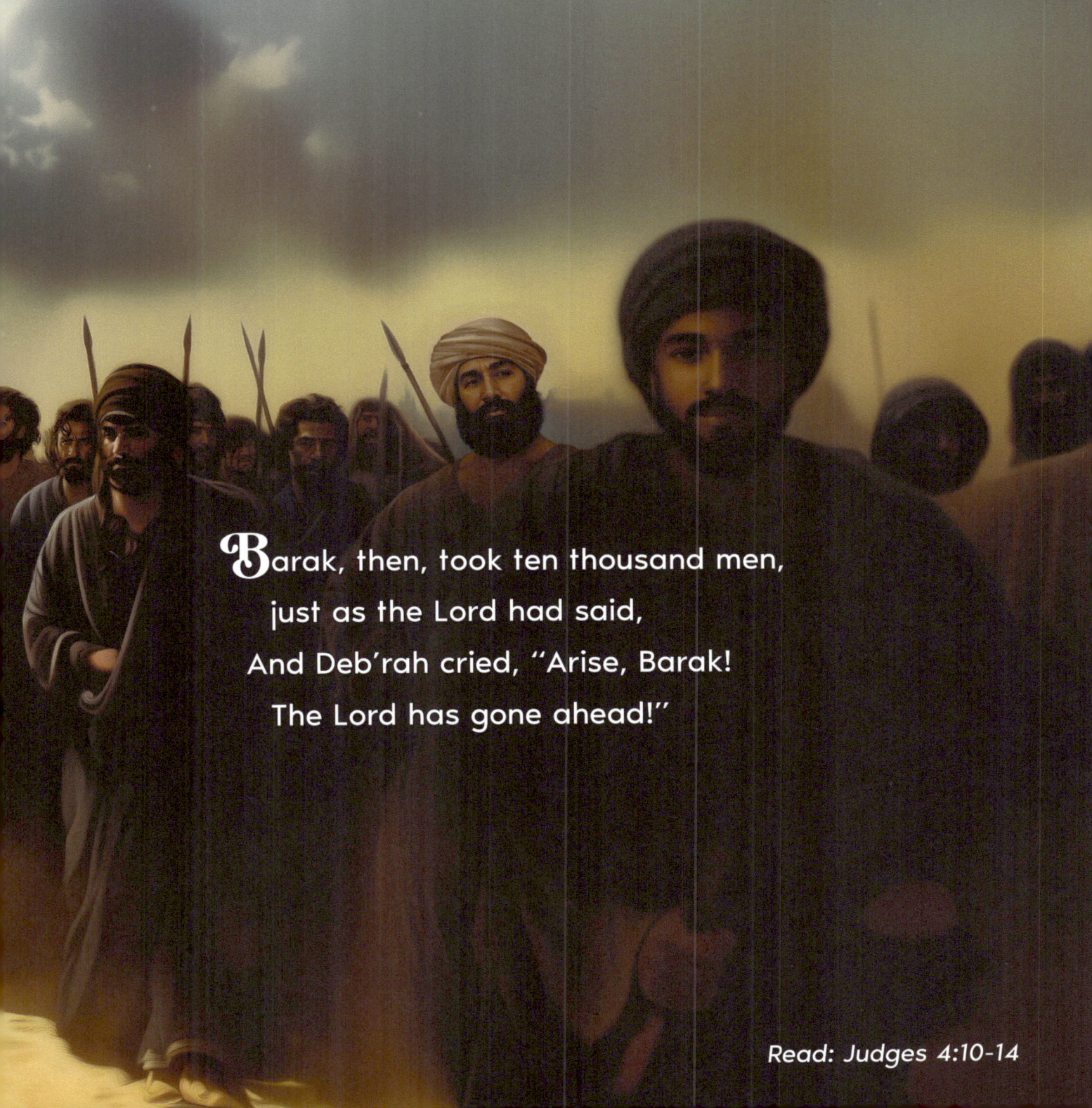

Barak, then, took ten thousand men,
just as the Lord had said,
And Deb'rah cried, "Arise, Barak!
The Lord has gone ahead!"

Read: Judges 4:10-14

Barak attacked, and Sisera's men fell that very day, And Sisera jumped from his chariot and ran away.

Read: Judges 4:15

He fled then to a woman's tent,
   a Kenite named Jael;
She said, "Come in, don't be afraid,
   in here you'll be quite well."

And Sisera said, "Give me water,
    quench my thirst so deep."
She brought him milk and covered him
    so he could fall asleep.

Read: Judges 4:17-20

And while he slept,
   Jael caused Sisera his fate to meet.

...Then moments later came Barak,
his triumph to complete.

And Jael said, "Come see the man
that you've been searching for.
He's been defeated by my hand—
he's done, he is no more!"

Read: Judges 4:21-22

Yes, on that day,
    God overpowered Jabin, Canaan's king;
The hand of Israel destroyed him,
    victory to bring.
Not by their power nor their might,
    but God who made them strong,
And in that day, Barak and Deb'rah
    broke into this song:

Read: Judges 4:23

Read: Judges 5:1-3

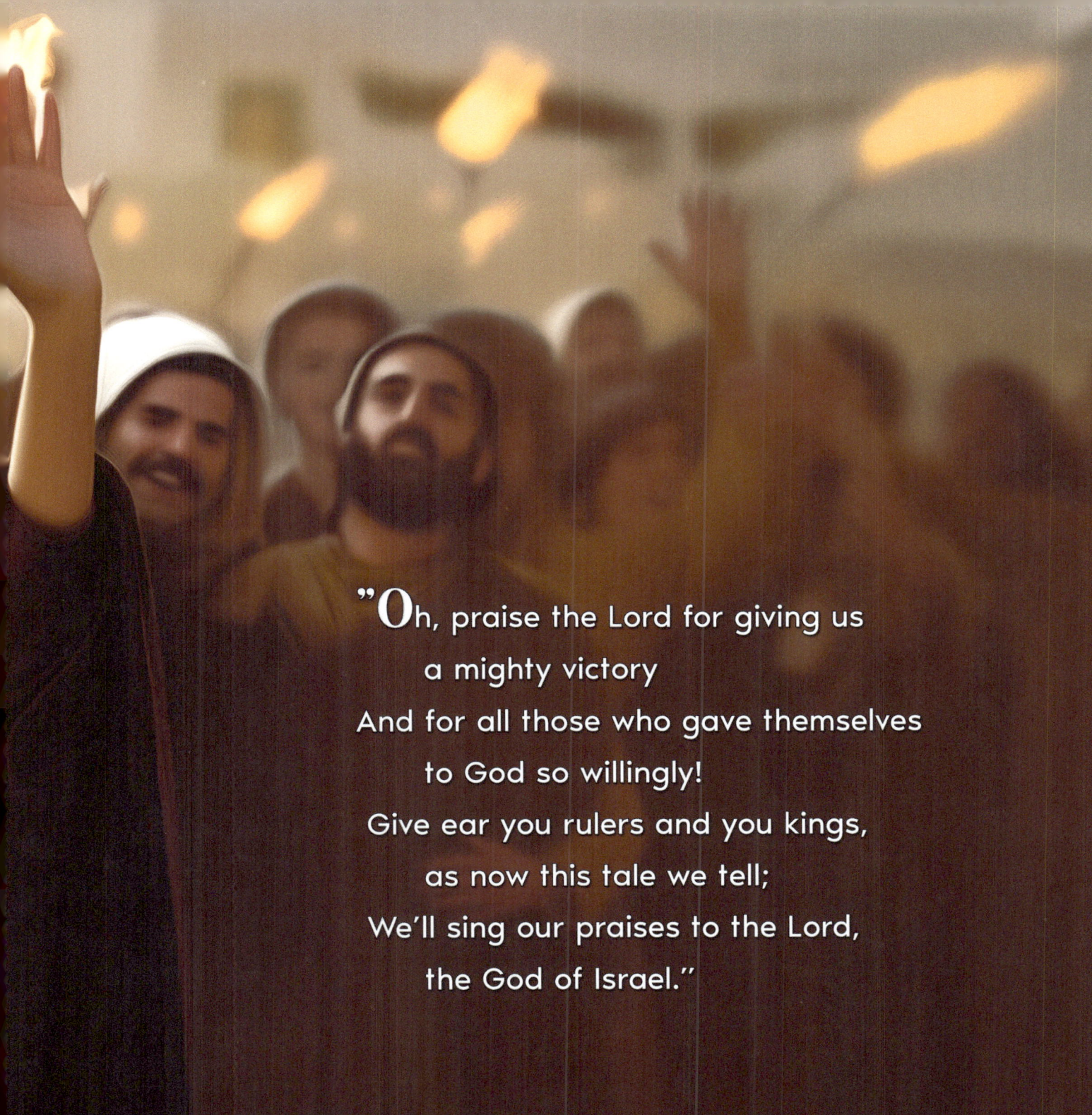

"Oh, praise the Lord for giving us
   a mighty victory
And for all those who gave themselves
   to God so willingly!
Give ear you rulers and you kings,
   as now this tale we tell;
We'll sing our praises to the Lord,
   the God of Israel."

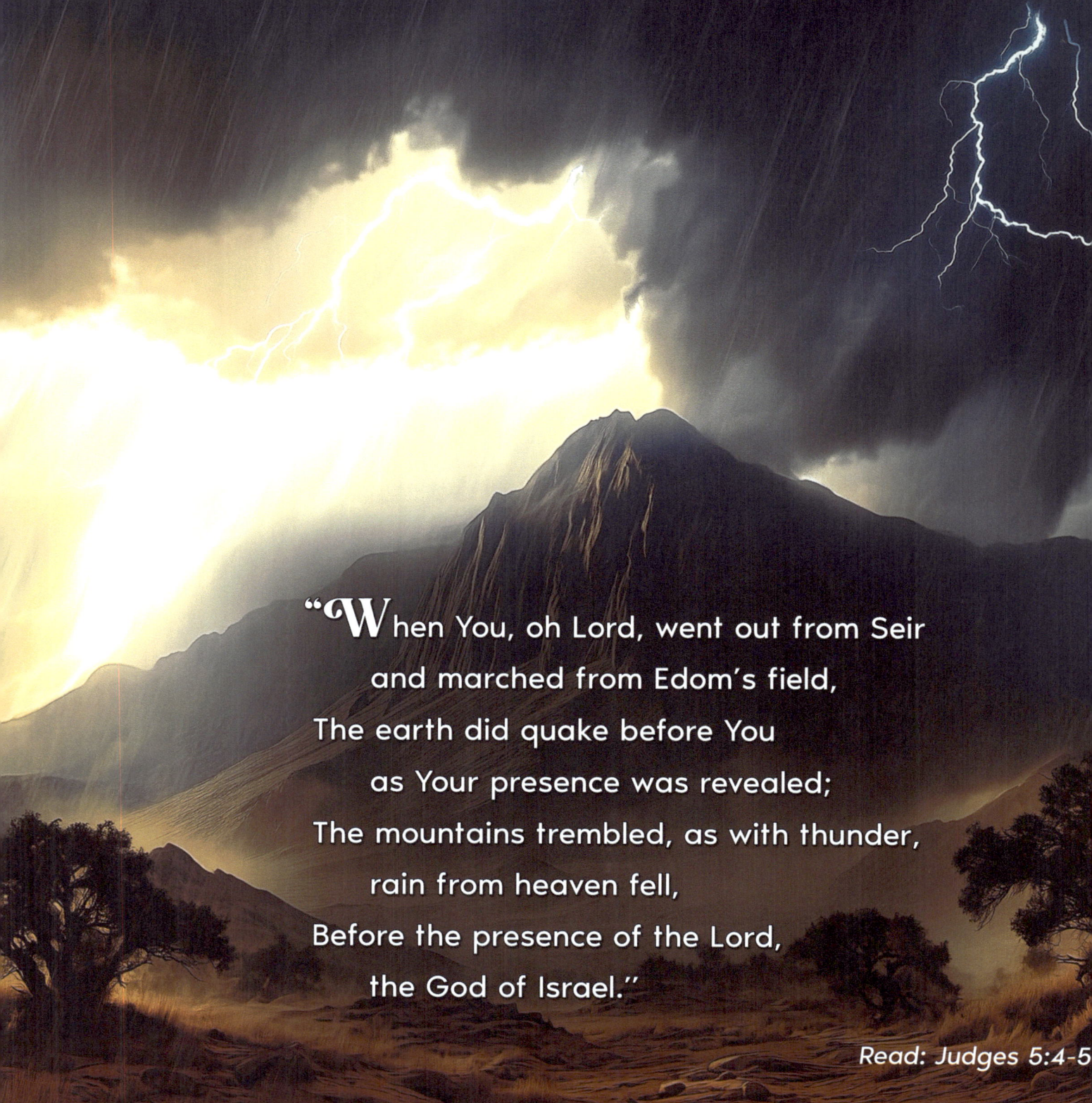

"When You, oh Lord, went out from Seir
and marched from Edom's field,
The earth did quake before You
as Your presence was revealed;
The mountains trembled, as with thunder,
rain from heaven fell,
Before the presence of the Lord,
the God of Israel."

Read: Judges 5:4-5

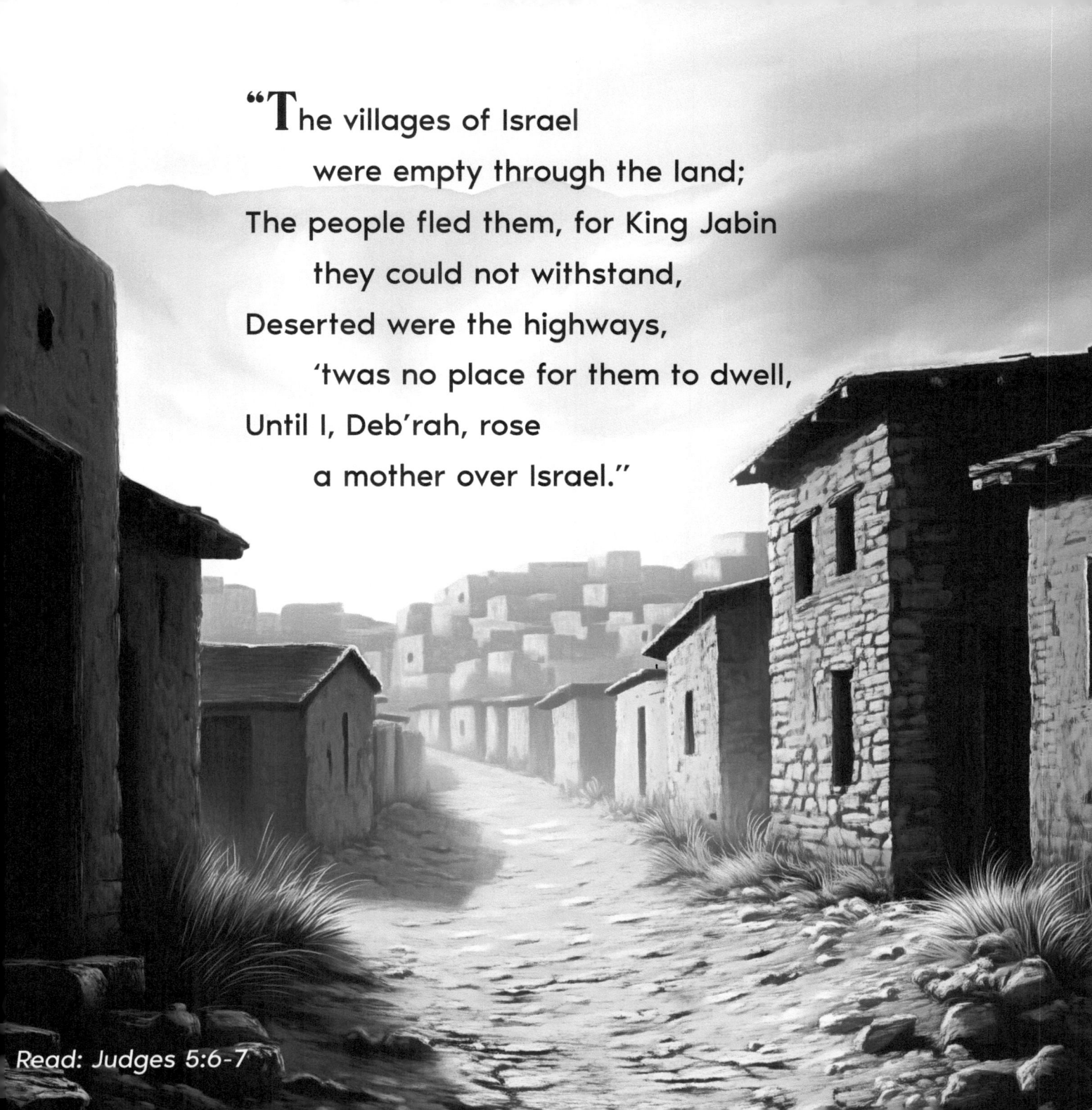

"The villages of Israel
   were empty through the land;
The people fled them, for King Jabin
   they could not withstand,
Deserted were the highways,
   'twas no place for them to dwell,
Until I, Deb'rah, rose
   a mother over Israel."

Read: Judges 5:6-7

"The people had done evil,
 loving things that God does hate,
Until the people rose
 and went down to the city gate.

Awake, awake, oh Deb'rah—
 oh, wake up, break out in song!
Arise, Barak, your captives take—
 oh, let your arm be strong!"

Read: Judges 5:11-12

"Then from the heavens far above, the stars joined in the fight; Opposing Sisera, they battled with celestial might.

"Oh Lord, defeat Your enemies,
the ones who've done us wrong;
But like the sun, may those who love You
rise forever strong.
As once again, we'll in this promised land
forever dwell;
We'll sing our praises to the Lord,
the God of Israel."

Read: Judges 5:31

So when you're facing troubles
    and you're tempted to despair;
With boldness take the lead
    and speak the Word of God in prayer.
Just trust in His great wisdom—
    He'll defeat the enemy;
Like Deb'rah, then, give Him
    the glory for His victory.

Discussion Guide

BOLD FAITH

Question: How did Deborah show bold faith in God?
Discuss: Deborah believed God's words and acted on them, even when the enemy seemed too strong. Bold faith means trusting God no matter what we see or feel. Ask your child when they've had to trust God for something even though they couldn't yet see it.

WISE LEADERSHIP

Question: What made Deborah a wise leader?
Discuss: Deborah listened to God and guided others with wisdom and truth. She didn't lead with pride but with courage and care for others. Talk with your child about what makes a good leader and how they can lead others to make wise choices.

ENCOURAGING OTHERS

Question: Why did Barak ask Deborah to go with him to battle?
Discuss: Barak felt stronger when Deborah came with him. She encouraged him with her presence and faith. Talk about how we can encourage others by standing with them and speaking truth when they feel afraid.

GOD'S POWER, NOT OURS

Question: Who really won the battle against Sisera and king Jabin?
Discuss: Even though Deborah, Barak, and Jael were brave, it was God who won the battle. God gave them victory, but He used Deborah, Barak, and Jael, each playing their part. Ask your child how they can rely on God's help when they face something hard.

UNEXPECTED HEROES

Question: Who defeated Sisera?
Discuss: God used Jael, an ordinary woman, in a big way. This shows that God can use anyone to do important things. Talk with your child about how God can use them too, no matter how small they feel.

PRAISING GOD

Question: What did Deborah and Barak do after the battle?
Discuss: They sang a song to praise God. It's important to give God the glory when He helps us. Ask your child how they like to praise God, through singing, prayer, or telling others what He's done.

LISTENING TO GOD

Question: How did Deborah know what to do?
Discuss: Deborah was a prophetess, which means she listened to God and shared His words. We can listen to God by reading the Bible, praying, and paying attention to what He might be showing us. Encourage your child to spend time with God and trust Him, especially when it is not clear what we should do.

GOD'S PURPOSE

Question: What was Deborah's special role in God's plan?
Discuss: God chose Deborah to lead and speak for Him. Just like Deborah, we all can be used by God.. Ask your child how they think God might want to use them.

ROLE MODEL

Question: If you could be like Deborah in one way, what would it be?
Discuss: Talk about Deborah's boldness, wisdom, and faith. Invite your child to choose a trait they admire and share how they can live it out in their own life, whether at school, at home, or with friends.

TO GET **FREE PRINTABLE DOWNLOADS**
of the Discussion Guide and other free resources,
GO TO MY **WEBSITE:** WWW.ARABELLAPENROSE.COM

About the Series

In a world filled with conflicting messages about femininity, the Real Women Heroes of the Bible series brings biblical role models to life for today's generation. Told in rhyming verse, each book tells of a different biblical heroine, showcasing their unique virtues and traits. The series features realistic illustrations that convey these are real women, not fairy tales. By exploring the lives of these women God intentionally chose to be featured in His Word, young girls can find godly examples of womanhood and be inspired to develop their own God-given strengths. Most importantly, they will understand that the very best models for what it means to be a woman can be found in the pages of the Bible. Each heroine's faith-filled life carries powerful lessons that will speak to the hearts of girls today.

COLLECT THE WHOLE SERIES!

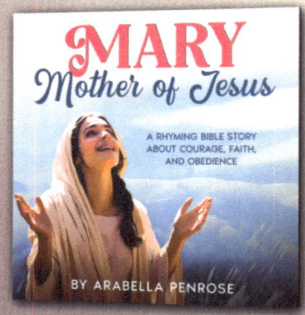 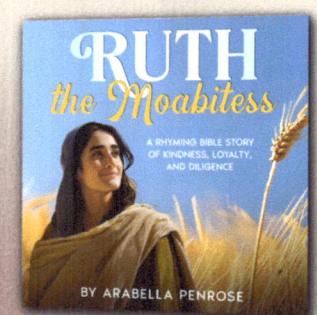 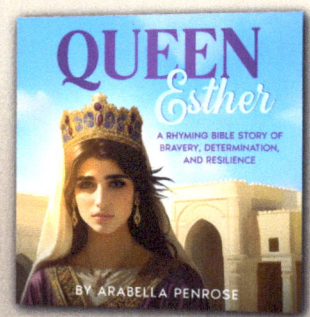 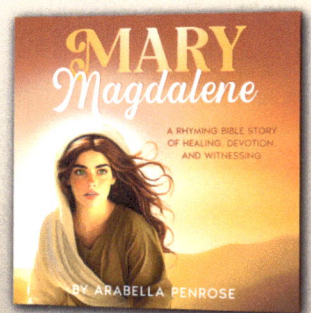

TO GET UPDATES ON NEW RELEASES,
sign up for my newsletter at www.arabellapenrose.com

About the Author

Since childhood, Arabella has always loved poetry and dreamed of one day publishing her own poems. She splits her time between her native Southern California and Southern Spain. After earning her Bachelor of Arts from UC Santa Barbara, Arabella worked as a translator and a teacher. But her true passion is to nurture the hearts of children through stories. In her spare time, you can find Arabella hiking or walking the beach with her pup, Snoopy, and spending time with her son, Mateo. Arabella draws inspiration from her father, who instilled in her a love of poetry and scripture. She hopes to glorify God with her stories and inspire the next generation to discover the transformative power of God's Word.

Thank You!

Dear reader,

I hope reading this rhyming bible story inspired you and your child as much as it did me in writing it.

If you found value in this book, please consider leaving an honest review on Amazon or Goodreads. Your feedback helps other families discover meaningful books. And, by sharing your thoughts, you encourage me to continue writing stories that nurture little hearts.

Thank you for reading this timeless tale of Deborah with your child. I'm grateful for readers like you.

Blessings,

Arabella Penrose

HAVE A PRAYER REQUEST
or want to reach out? Email me at
arabella@arabellapenrose.com

www.ingramcontent.com/pod-product-compliance
Lightning Source LLC
Chambersburg PA
CBHW041406010526
44107CB00015B/1086